AF228865

IN FOCUS...
GROSS BUGS
CAMILLA DE LA BÉDOYÈRE
Quarto Library

Quarto is the authority on a wide range of topics.

Quarto educates, entertains and enriches the lives of our readers—enthusiasts and lovers of hands-on living.

www.quartoknows.com

This library edition published in 2019
by Quarto Library,
an imprint of The Quarto Group.
6 Orchard Road
Suite 100
Lake Forest, CA 92630
T: +1 949 380 7510
F: +1 949 380 7575
www.QuartoKnows.com

Distributed in the United States and Canada by
Lerner Publisher Services
241 First Avenue North
Minneapolis, MN 55401 U.S.A.
www.lernerbooks.com

A CIP record for this book is available from
the Library of Congress.

ISBN 978 0 7112 4804 5

Manufactured in Guangdong, China CC072019

9 8 7 6 5 4 3 2 1

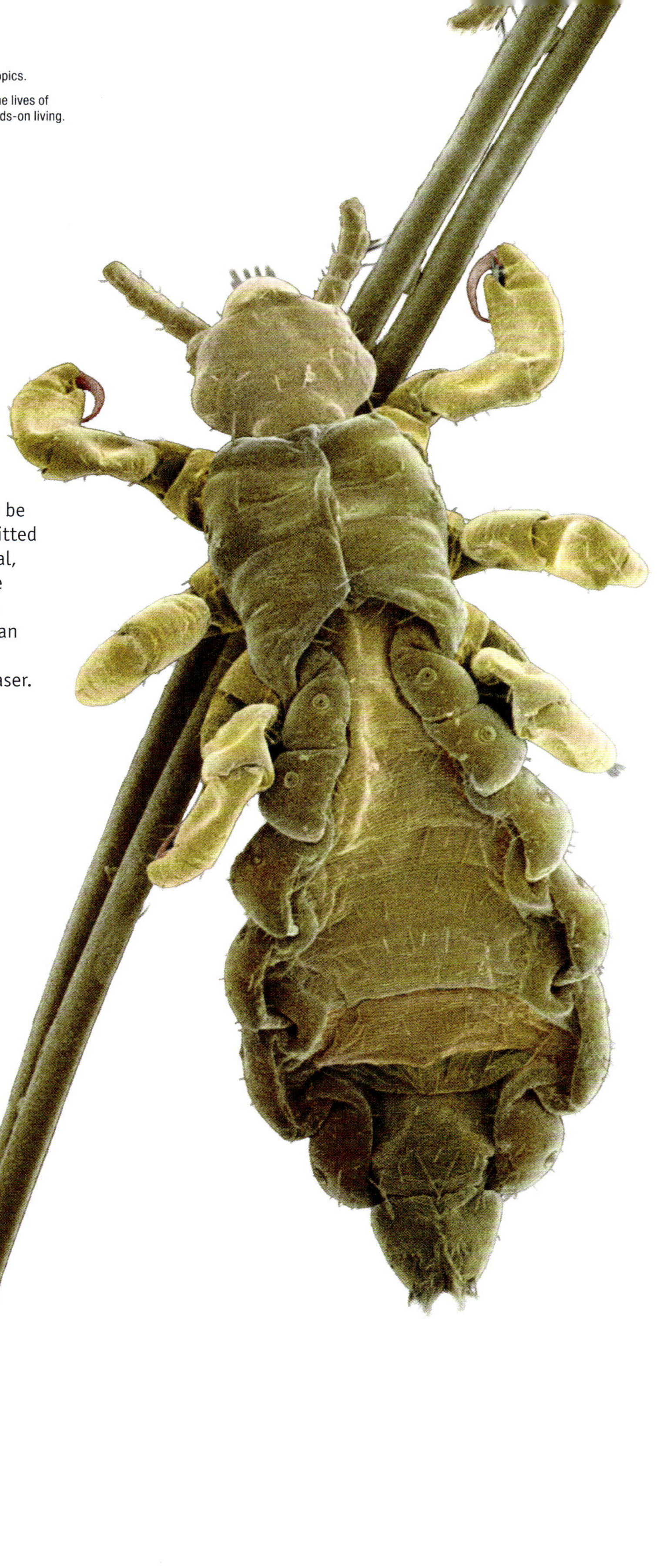

CONTENTS

INTRODUCTION...................................... 4

EARWIGS AND COCKROACHES 6

FLIES 8

FLEAS AND SCORPIONFLIES 10

TERMITES 12

LICE AND THRIPS 14

SHORT-HORNED FLIES 16

MORE SHORT-HORNED FLIES 18

MITES AND TICKS 20

TRUE BUGS 22

LONG-HORNED FLIES 24

SAWFLIES, WOOD WASPS, AND

HORNTAILS....................................... 26

BUG WORLD 28

GLOSSARY... 31

INDEX.. 32

INTRODUCTION

Bugs, mini-monsters, or creepy-crawlies—these creatures have many names. They belong to a huge group of animals called **invertebrates**, and they live all over the world. The most successful invertebrates are **insects**. One reason for their success is that insects are able to eat a wide range of foods, from leaves to blood and even each other!

What is an insect?

Insects have bodies that are divided into three parts: a head, a **thorax**, and an **abdomen**. Three pairs of legs are attached to the thorax, and many insects have one or two pairs of wings as well. The abdomen contains the body parts that digest food. Insects do not have blood. They have a liquid called hemolymph instead.

A giant swallowtail butterfly larva has a gross way of staying safe-it looks like bird poop! This puts birds off trying to eat it.

Baby bugs

Most insects start life as an egg that is laid by their mother somewhere safe. When it hatches, the young insect emerges as a soft-bodied larva or nymph. Young insects often look very different from the adults, and live in different habitats and eat different foods. When the young adult has grown enough, it will change into an adult. Some insects become a **pupa** while they go through these changes.

Female mosquitoes are flies that need a blood meal before they can lay their eggs. As they feed, the abdomen swells and turns red.

It looks revolting when young, but an adult giant swallowtail is transformed into a beautiful butterfly.

Types of insect

Scientists who study insects have found about one million **species** so far, but there are lots more to discover. Insects make their homes everywhere, from the sunlit tops of rainforest trees to half-frozen soil around the Arctic. Insects are divided into groups such as beetles, flies, and true bugs.

EARWIGS AND COCKROACHES

Cockroaches are one of the most ancient groups of insects. They have existed for more than 350 million years. They live in many different habitats, from mountains to tropical rainforests. A few species live in buildings and are considered pests. Earwigs feed on plants and flowers and can also be pests. Their flat bodies make it easy for them to crawl into small hiding places.

American cockroach

This insect is found all over the world. It usually stays hidden during the day and comes out at night to eat. It will eat a wide range of things, including paper, hair, cloth, and almost anything that is rotting.

American cockroaches are attracted to sweet foods, such as apple.

Common earwig

The common earwig has short wings, a long shiny body, and a forked tail. The female lays her eggs in a nest under a stone or log. Unusually for an insect, she stays near the nest to protect the eggs and lick them clean. She also looks after the young until they are able to feed themselves.

Madagascar hissing cockroach

When alarmed, this large cockroach makes a loud, hissing sound through breathing holes in its abdomen. Males also hiss when they are fighting each other. They usually live in forests. Some people keep them as pets.

FLIES

Flies are one of the largest insect groups. There are more than 124,000 known species. After bees and wasps, flies are the most important **pollinators** of **crops**, and they also help get rid of rotting waste. This chapter also looks at scorpionflies and fleas.

Maggots like to feed on rotting food.

Life cycle

House flies, and many other flies, have a four-stage life cycle. First the female lays her eggs. The larvae, known as maggots, hatch from the eggs after 8 to 20 hours. After 4 to 10 days, the maggots start the pupa stage of their life. They develop a reddish-brown skin, and inside this they turn into a full-grown adult with wings.

Eyes

A fly's large eyes are made up of thousands of tiny lenses. These are good at seeing quick movements, but are not so good at seeing slow-moving things.

One pair of wings

Unlike most insects, flies have one pair of wings instead of two. A fly's wings beat up to 200 times a second, allowing it to hover and even fly backward as well as forward. The wings stop as soon as the fly's feet touch down.

FLEAS AND SCORPIONFLIES

Fleas and scorpionflies are not true flies. Fleas are tiny, wingless insects that feed on the blood of birds and other creatures. Scorpionflies belong to a separate group. They have large jaws and long, narrow wings.

Scorpionflies

Scorpionflies usually live in woodland or forests, where they feed on dead insects. Sometimes they steal trapped **prey** from a spider's web. The female lays her eggs on the ground. When they hatch, the larvae also hunt for dead insects to eat.

Oriental rat flea

This common flea lives on the blood of rats and humans, as well as other animals. It can spread disease if it bites a human after biting an infected rat.

Cat flea

Although this type of flea usually lives on cats, it can also live on dogs. It has long, powerful back legs that help it to jump onto the animal to feed. Females lay their eggs in a cat's bedding, and the larvae eat waste from the adult fleas.

TERMITES

Termites live together in huge groups, called colonies. They spend most of their time in their nests, built either underground or in trees or mounds. Their small, soft bodies are quite fragile, and they can die after just a few hours in the open air. Most of the termites in a **colony** are blind **workers** that have no wings. They build the nest and look after the **queen** and the larvae. The queen has her own **cell** in the nest, where she lives with her **mate.** Her only task is to lay eggs. At certain times of the year, special termites with wings and eyes leave the colony and fly away to set up new colonies of their own.

12

Eating wood

Many termite species feed on wood. They have special germs in their stomach that break down this tough food. Some species of wood-eating termite are thought of as a serious pest.

Wood-eating termites eat the wood of buildings, furniture, and stored timber.

Some termites build huge mounds from mud where large colonies live together. They can be more than 6 feet (1.8 meters) tall!

FOUL FACT

Termite colonies eat non-stop, 24 hours a day, seven days a week!

Soldiers

Most termite colonies include special soldier termites that defend the nest against attacks from enemies, such as ants. Some types of soldier termites have bigger heads and jaws than the workers. Others, such as the snouted termite, can spray a sticky, nasty-smelling liquid at their enemies.

13

LICE AND THRIPS

Lice are small, wingless insects that live as **parasites** on other creatures. There are two main types—sucking lice and chewing lice. Thrips are related to lice, but are not parasites.

Rose thrips feed and lay their eggs deep inside a rose bud or flower.

Thrips

There are as many as 5,000 species of thrips. Some are pests of particular plants or crops. These tiny bugs pierce leaves or flowers and suck up the plant juices.

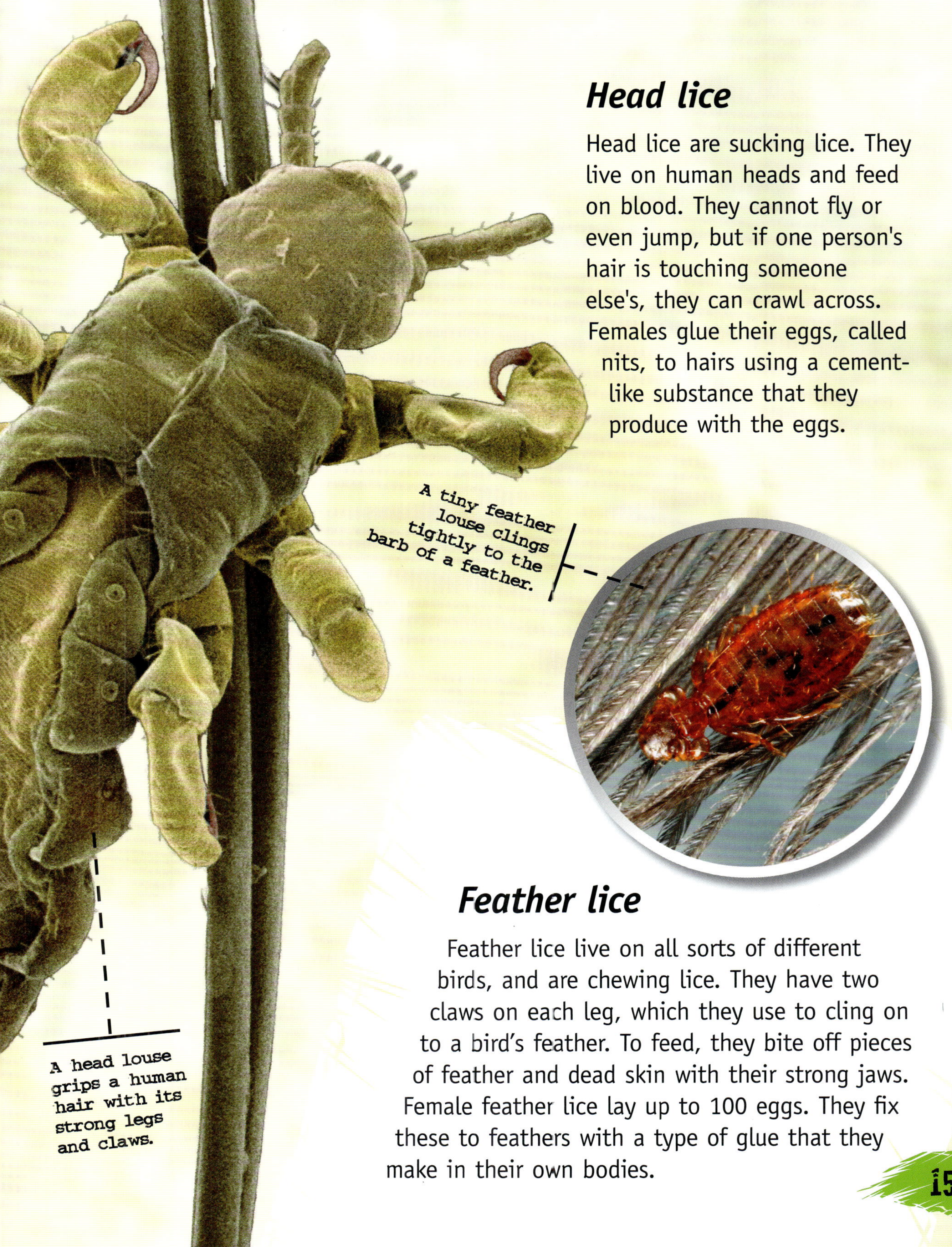

Head lice

Head lice are sucking lice. They live on human heads and feed on blood. They cannot fly or even jump, but if one person's hair is touching someone else's, they can crawl across. Females glue their eggs, called nits, to hairs using a cement-like substance that they produce with the eggs.

A tiny feather louse clings tightly to the barb of a feather.

Feather lice

Feather lice live on all sorts of different birds, and are chewing lice. They have two claws on each leg, which they use to cling on to a bird's feather. To feed, they bite off pieces of feather and dead skin with their strong jaws. Female feather lice lay up to 100 eggs. They fix these to feathers with a type of glue that they make in their own bodies.

A head louse grips a human hair with its strong legs and claws.

SHORT-HORNED FLIES

Short-horned flies, such as horse flies, have bigger bodies and shorter **antennae** than long-horned flies.

Horse flies

Female horse flies feed on the blood of animals, including humans. They make a small cut on their victim, then lick up the blood as it flows. Their bites are painful, and the flies can carry diseases.

A tiny common bee fly adult feeds on a forget-me-not flower.

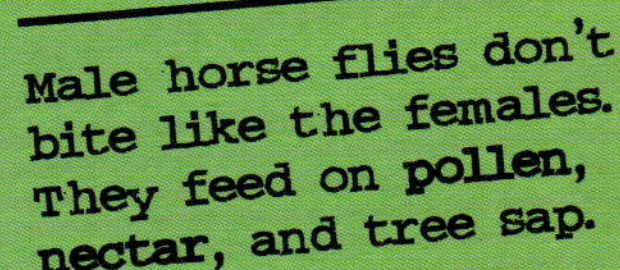

Male horse flies don't bite like the females. They feed on **pollen**, **nectar**, and tree sap.

Bee flies

These stout, hairy flies look like bees, and some behave like bees, too. They hover in front of flowers, feeding on nectar by sucking it up with their mouthparts.

Robber flies

There are about 5,500 species of robber fly.
These fast-moving hunters chase and catch
other insects, in the air or on the ground.
Once a robber fly has caught its victim, it
uses its short, sharp mouthparts to suck out
the liquid in the insect's body.

MORE SHORT-HORNED FLIES

Some short-horned flies feed and lay their eggs on dung and dead animals. This might not sound nice, but these insects perform a useful job by recycling this rotting material.

Blow flies

Blow flies include blue bottles and green bottles, which have bodies that shine like polished metal. Adult blow flies feed on pollen and nectar, as well as anything that is rotting. Many species lay their eggs in dung, or in the bodies of dead animals, so the larvae can feed as soon as they hatch.

Blow fly females eat dung because it is full of protein, which they need to lay eggs.

A house fly's long, strawlike mouthparts have a spongy "sucker" at the end.

House fly

The house fly feeds on garbage and animal dung. It can only eat by mopping up liquid food. When it lands on something that it wants to eat, it spits on the food first. This helps to break it down, so the fly can soak it up.

Dung fly

The dung fly preys on other insects, including flies. The female lays her eggs on cattle dung, while the male guards the patch of dung from other males. When the larvae hatch, they feed on the dung.

FOUL FACT

Female house flies can lay up to 500 eggs in a few days. It takes less than two weeks for each one to become an adult fly.

A male yellow dung fly protects the female as she lays her eggs in fresh dung.

19

MITES AND TICKS

Mites and ticks are the smallest **arachnids**. They live almost everywhere, in hot and cold places and even in the sea. Ticks feed on the blood of animals.

Hard tick larvae have six legs when they first hatch. They then grow into **nymphs** with eight legs.

Adult house mites measure just 0.2 inches (5 millimeters).

House-dust mites

These tiny mites are common in houses all over the world. They feed on the tiny pieces of skin found in house dust. Their droppings can sometimes cause allergies and make people unwell.

Hard ticks

Hard ticks cling to plant stems and climb on to any animal that brushes past. The tick holds on to the animal with its strong mouthparts and feeds on its blood for 5 to 7 days. Some species spread diseases as they feed.

Velvet mites

These mites are common in soil and moss, and on walls. Adult velvet mites feed mostly on insect eggs. Their larvae feed as parasites on insects and spiders.

TRUE BUGS

There are about 90,000 species of true bugs. All have sucking mouthparts, which they can swing forward to reach a greater range of foods.

Plantbugs

Plantbugs are the biggest family of true bugs. They live all over the world. Most of them feed on leaves, seeds, and fruit, but some are serious pests, eating crops such as cotton and tea.

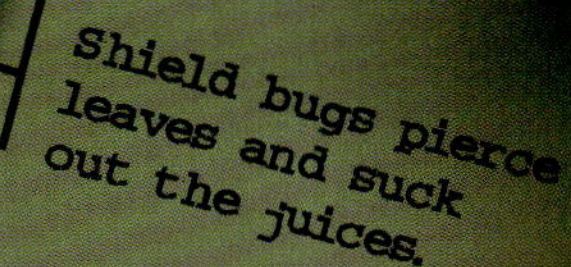

Shield bugs pierce leaves and suck out the juices.

Assassin bugs

Fierce-looking assassin bugs attack and kill other insects, such as caterpillars, beetles, bees, and other bugs. Once they have caught their prey, they inject it with spit. This stops the insect from moving, and the assassin then sucks up all of its victim's body juices.

Stinkbugs

These bugs are named for the nasty-smelling liquid that they spray over attackers. Most **predators** run away as soon as they smell it. A stinkbug's mouthparts are inside its beak-shaped snout. It uses them to stab plants, so that it can suck up the sap inside.

The smelly liquid that a stinkbug uses to warn off predators comes from two stink organs underneath its body.

An assassin bug uses its long mouthparts to inject venom (a poisonous liquid) into a stink or shield bug.

23

LONG-HORNED FLIES

The family of true flies is split into two groups, long-horned flies and short-horned flies. Long-horned flies usually have small bodies, long antennae, and long, thin legs. They include crane flies, mosquitoes, and midges.

Mosquitoes

You can usually hear a mosquito before you see it. Its wings beat so fast that it makes a whining noise as it flies. Most female mosquitoes bite animals with their long mouthparts, or "stinger," and suck their blood. In some countries, mosquitoes spread dangerous diseases.

Midges and biting midges

Midges are tiny insects that do not bite. They fly in huge swarms and are often seen near ponds and streams. Biting midges belong to a separate family. Also known as punkies or no-see-ums, these tiny insects can give a painful bite. Some of them bite humans and suck their blood, and others feed on insects.

FOUL FACT

Crane flies are also known as gollywhoppers, skeeter eaters and gallnippers! Their larvae are sometimes called leatherjackets.

Crane flies

Crane flies are one of the largest fly families. These insects have long, thin legs and fragile bodies. Adult crane flies live for only a few days. Some feed on nectar, but most don't eat at all. The larvae mainly feed on plants, although some are predators.

25

SAWFLIES, WOOD WASPS, AND HORNTAILS

Sawflies get their name from the saw-like egg-laying tube of the female. The adults look like wasps, but without the narrow "waist" between the thorax and abdomen. Their larvae look like fat, hairless caterpillars.

A wood wasp makes a hole in a rotten pine log, where she will lay her eggs.

FOUL FACT

The larvae of some types of sawfly "talk" to each other, by making tapping noises with their tails.

Parasitic wood wasps

Unlike other sawflies, the larvae of parasitic wood wasps do not feed on plants. The female lays her eggs in the nest of other insects, such as wood-boring beetles and horntails. When the wood wasp larvae hatch, they kill and eat the other larvae in the nest.

Horntails

These wasp-like insects are named for the spike at the end of their body. They usually lay their eggs on conifer trees. When the larvae hatch, they burrow into the tree and can live inside for up to two years.

Common sawflies

This is the largest family of sawflies. The female uses her egg-laying tube to cut slits in the stems and leaves of plants. She then lays her eggs inside. The larvae feed on the leaves when they hatch.

BUG WORLD

Many insects look gross, and just as many have gross lifestyles, but they have important jobs to do in nature. Without them, the balance of animals and plants in the world would change forever.

This ugly bug is the larva of a ladybug. It feeds on **aphids**, which can damage plants, so it does an important job.

Pollination

Insects pollinate plants. This means they carry pollen from one flower to another, where it fertilises flower eggs. Once the eggs have been fertilised, the plants can grow seeds, nuts, and fruit, which are food for billions of animals, including humans.

Many adult tachinid flies feed on pollen. They are important pollinators in mountainous areas, where bees are few.

Nature's recyclers

Many insects and bugs feast on rotting plants and animals, and even dung. These small creatures help to keep the planet free from waste and disease. They recycle the goodness in dead plants and animals and dung, and turn it back into nutrients in the soil. These nutrients make the soil fertile, so new plants can grow.

Big plant-eaters such as elephants make huge amounts of dung. Dung beetles feed their larvae with the dung. This recycles the waste and fertilizes the soil

Zoom in

Learning more about insects and how they live is easy because they are all around us—even in our homes! A small hand lens, or a magnifying glass, is a useful piece of equipment for zooming in on an insect when it is feeding on a plant. Look for its three body parts, and count how many legs and wings it has. Always take care around insects, as some of them sting or bite.

PICTURE CREDITS

BC = back cover, FC = front cover, b = bottom, c = center, t = top, l = left, r = right

Alamy: 4-5 Phil Degginger; 14l Nigel Cattlin; 15r blickwinkel; 20-21 Razvan Cornel Constantin; 28cl Avico Ltd.

FLPA (www.flpa.co.uk) and its associate agencies: 1 Chien Lee/Minden Pictures; 2 Albert Lleal/Minden Pictures; 6br Nigel Cattlin; 7tl Hans Lang/Imagebroker; 8-9 Murray Cooper/Minden Pictures; 9tr Michael Durham/Minden Pictures; 10-11 Matt Cole; 11tl pd (Centers for Disease Control and Prevention's Public Health Image Library); 11br Â© Biosphoto , Christian Gautier/Biosphoto; 12br Mitsuhiko Imamori/Minden Pictures; 14-15 Albert Lleal/Minden Pictures; 16bl Roger Tidman; 16tr Martin B Withers; 17 Chien Lee/Minden Pictures; 18bl Erica Olsen; 18-19 Nigel Cattlin; 19br Richard Becker; 20l Nigel Cattlin; 21tl Dietmar Nill/Minden Pictures; 23tr Pete Oxford/Minden Pictures; 24c Mark Moffett/Minden Pictures; 24-25 Derek Middleton; 26-27 Gianpiero Ferrari; 27tl Derek Middleton; 27c Thomas Marent/Minden Pictures; 30 10-11 Matt Cole

Shutterstock.com: FC Shutter Rich; BC Cornel Constantin; 5bl JM Estes; 5tr BeanRibbon; 6-7 Vladimir Wrangel; 8cl Roman Kutsekon; 12-13 sydeen; 13cl Piotr Gatlik; 22bl Maciej Olszewski; 22-23 Steve Heap; 25tr Lee Hua Ming; 28-29 Nata Naumovec; 29cr efendy

GLOSSARY

abdomen
back end of an insect's body, attached to the thorax

antennae
two long, thin feelers on an insect's head that help the insect to smell, taste, and touch things

aphids
tiny insects that feed by sucking nectar from plants

arachnids
creatures with a 2-part body and 8 jointed legs. Spiders, scorpions, ticks, and mites are arachnids

cell
a very small, 6-sided "room" in the nest of a bee or wasp, used for storing food or eggs

colony
a group of same-species insects living together in one place. Ants, termites, and some bee and wasp species live in colonies

crops
plants, such as wheat, grown by farmers for people to eat

disease
an illness that prevents the body from working normally

insects
animals with a head, thorax, abdomen, 3 pairs of legs attached to the thorax, and 1 or 2 pairs of wings

invertebrates
animals with no backbone

larva/larvae
an insect's young, after it has hatched from an egg and before it becomes an adult

mate
one of a pair of animals that has chosen another to produce young

mites
tiny creatures related to spiders and ticks

nectar
the sugary liquid produced by many flowers

nymphs
the young or larval stage of some insects, such as grasshoppers

parasites
animals or plants that live on other animals or plants

pollen
a powder produced by the male part of a flower. Pollen makes the female part of a flower produce seeds. It is usually yellow.

pollinators
insects that carry pollen from one flower to another, helping them to produce seeds

predators
animals that hunt and kill other animals for food

prey
an animal that is hunted and eaten by another animal

pupa
a stage in the life cycle of some insects when the insect changes from a larva into an adult

queen
an egg-laying female in a colony of ants, bees, wasps, or termites

species
a group of animals with similar characteristics. Animals of the same species can mate and produce young

thorax
the part of an insect's body between the head and abdomen

workers
the insects in a colony that build the nest, find food, and care for young

INDEX

abdomen 4, 5, 7, 31
allergies 20
American cockroaches 6
antennae 16, 24, 25, 31
ants 13
aphids 28, 31
arachnids 20, 31
assassin bugs 22, 23

bee flies 16, 17
bees 8, 15, 22
beetles 5, 22, 26, 29
biting midges 25
bloodsuckers 5, 10, 11, 15, 16,
    20, 21, 24, 25
blow flies 18
blue bottles 18
body parts 4
bugs, true 5, 22–23, 28, 29

cat fleas 11
chewing lice 14
cockroaches 6
colonies 12, 13, 31
common earwigs 7
common sawflies 27
crane flies 24, 25

diseases 10, 11, 16, 21, 24, 31
dung beetles 29
dung flies 19

earwigs 6–7
eggs 5, 7, 8, 10, 11, 12, 14, 15,
    18, 19, 21, 26, 27, 28

eyes 9, 17

feather lice 15
fleas 10, 11
flies 5, 8–9, 16–19, 24–25, 26,
    27, 28
fruit flies 9

giant swallowtail butterflies 4–5
green bottles 18

hard ticks 20, 21
head lice 15
hemolymph 4
horntails 26, 27
horse flies 9, 16
house flies 8, 18, 19
house-dust mites 20

insect species, number of 5
invertebrates 4, 31

jaws 10, 13, 15

ladybugs 28
larvae 4, 5, 8, 10, 11, 12, 17,
    18, 19, 20, 25, 26, 27, 28,
    29, 31
lice 14–15
life cycle 8
long-horned earwigs 7
long-horned flies 24–25

Madagascar hissing cockroaches 7
maggots 8
midges 24, 25
mites 20–21, 31
mosquitoes 5, 24

nests 7, 12, 13
nits 15

nymphs 5, 20, 31

Oriental rat fleas 11

parasites 14, 21, 26, 31
pests 6, 13, 14, 22
pincers 7
plantbugs 22
pollinators 8, 28, 31
pupae 5, 8, 31

queens 12, 31

rat fleas 10, 11
robber flies 17
rose thrips 14

sawflies 26, 27
scorpionflies 10
shield bugs 22
short-horned flies 16–19, 24
snouted termites 13
soldiers 13
"stingers" 24
stinkbugs 23
sucking lice 14, 15

tachinid flies 28
termites 12–13
thorax 4, 31
thrips 14–15
ticks 20–21

velvet mites 21
venom 23

wasps 8, 26
wings 4, 8, 9, 10, 24
wood wasps 26
wood-boring beetles 26
wood-eating termites 13
workers 12, 31